Proteins

By Justine and Ron Fontes

Consultants

Reading Adviser
Nanci R. Vargus, EdD
Assistant Professor of Literacy
University of Indianapolis, Indianapolis, Indiana

Subject Adviser
Janet M. Gilchrist, PhD, RD
Nutritionist

Children's Press®
A Division of Scholastic Inc.
New York Toronto London Auckland Sydney
Mexico City New Delhi Hong Kong
Danbury, Connecticut

Designer: Herman Adler Design
Photo Researcher: Caroline Anderson
The photo on the cover shows different sources of protein.

Library of Congress Cataloging-in-Publication Data

Fontes, Justine.
  Proteins / by Justine and Ron Fontes.
      p. cm. — (Rookie read-about health)
  Includes index.
  ISBN 0-516-23647-4 (lib. bdg.)   0-516-24650-X (pbk.)
  1. Proteins in human nutrition—Juvenile literature. 2. Food—Protein
content—Juvenile literature. I. Fontes, Ron. II. Title. III. Series.
  TX553.P7F65 2005
  613.2'82—dc22   2005004778

CHILDREN'S PRESS, and ROOKIE READ-ABOUT®,
and associated logos are trademarks and/or registered trademarks
of Scholastic Library Publishing. SCHOLASTIC and associated logos
are trademarks and/or registered trademarks of Scholastic Inc.

1 2 3 4 5 6 7 8 9 10 R 14 13 12 11 10 09 08 07 06 05

Did you know that your body is made of protein? Proteins are the building blocks of all living things.

Your body gets protein
from the foods you eat.

What foods on this table
have protein in them?

6

Some protein comes from animals. Meat, fish, eggs, milk, and cheese all have animal proteins.

Some protein comes from plants. Nuts, beans, and peas have plant proteins. So do certain breads and cereals.

9

Protein builds muscles.
Muscles help you move
by pulling your bones.

Every organ in your body is made of protein. An organ is a body part that has a special job.

The heart is an organ that pumps blood through the body.

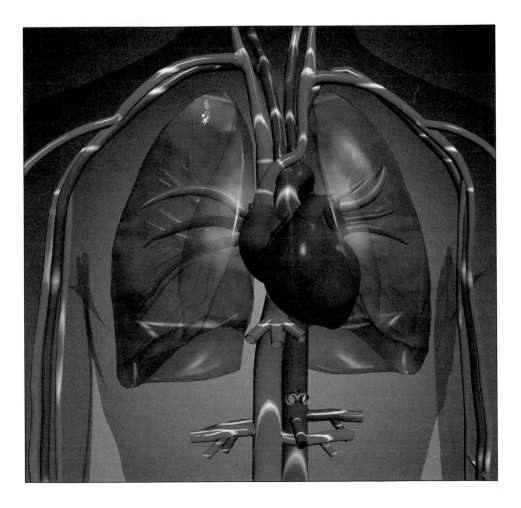

Protein is used to make skin, hair, and bones. It replaces body parts that get hurt.

Protein also helps your body fight sickness.

Protein is used to make hormones. Hormones give your body important messages. One hormone tells your body to grow.

Hormones travel in your blood. Protein is used to make blood, too!

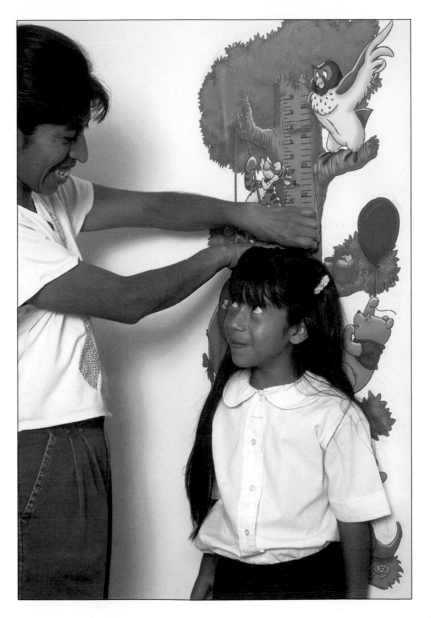

17

18

But how does your body make its own protein?

First, it breaks down the animal and plant proteins in the foods you eat.

Then, it builds the new proteins you need.

Amino acids are the building blocks of all proteins. There are twenty different amino acids.

Your body can put them together in many different ways. It can use them to build thousands of different proteins.

Your body can make eleven amino acids.

You need to get the other nine from the foods you eat. These nine are called essential amino acids.

Animal proteins are "complete." They have all nine essential amino acids.

24

Most plant proteins are "incomplete." They don't have all nine essential amino acids.

Eating enough different plant proteins together can solve this problem. Together, rice and beans make a complete protein.

Scientists came up with the Food Guidance System. It tells you how many times a day you should eat different types of food to stay healthy.

Be sure to eat foods with protein at least twice a day!

MyPyramid.gov
STEPS TO A HEALTHIER YOU

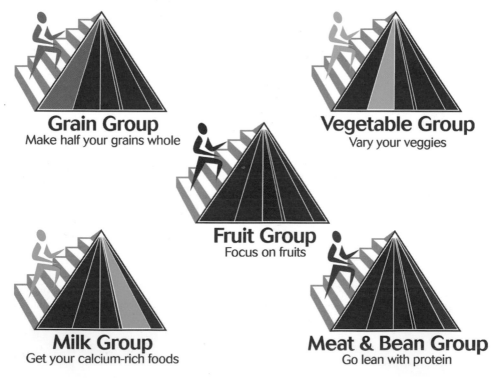

Grain Group
Make half your grains whole

Vegetable Group
Vary your veggies

Fruit Group
Focus on fruits

Milk Group
Get your calcium-rich foods

Meat & Bean Group
Go lean with protein

Protein isn't all your body needs to stay healthy, but it's a good start!

Words You Know

bread

eggs

hair

meat

30

milk

muscle

nuts

peas

Index

About the Author

Justine and Ron Fontes have written many books for children. They live with three cats in Maine, where they enjoy reading, writing, drawing, juggling, and making movies. They also like cooking, gardening, critter watching, playing ping-pong, and trying new things.

Photo Credits

Photographs © 2005: Corbis Images: 14, 30 bottom left (Roy Morsch), 3 (Royalty-Free), 28 (David Thomas/PictureArts); Envision Stock Photography Inc.: 6 bottom right (Mark Ferri), cover, 6 top left, 9 top left, 24, 30 bottom right, 31 bottom left (Steven Needham); PhotoEdit: 17 (Bill Aron), 5 (Richard Hutchings), 6 top right, 30 top right (Michael Newman), 10, 31 top right (Patrick O'Lear), 23 (David Young-Wolff); photolibrary.com/Eisenhut & Mayer: 9 bottom left, 31 bottom right; PictureQuest/Bananastock, Ltd.: 18; James Levin/Studio 10: 20; Superstock, Inc.: 9 top right (Catherine de Torquat/Stock Food), 13 (Hank Grebe), 6 bottom left, 31 top left (Sucre Sale), 9 bottom right, 30 top left.